LITERATURE FROM CRESCENT MOON PUBLISHING

Sexing Hardy: Thomas Hardy and Feminism
by Margaret Elvy

Thomas Hardy's Jude the Obscure: A Critical Study
by Margaret Elvy

Thomas Hardy's Tess of the d'Urbervilles: A Critical Study
by Margaret Elvy

Stepping Forward: Essays, Lectures and Interviews
by Wolfgang Iser

Andrea Dworkin
by Jeremy Mark Robinson

German Romantic Poetry: Goethe, Novalis, Heine, Hölderlin
by Carol Appleby

Cavafy: Anatomy of a Soul
by Matt Crispin

Rilke: Space, Essence and Angels in the Poetry of Rainer Maria Rilke
by B.D. Barnacle

Rimbaud: Arthur Rimbaud and the Magic of Poetry
by Jeremy Mark Robinson

Shakespeare: Love, Poetry and Magic in Shakespeare's Sonnets and Plays
by B.D. Barnacle

Feminism and Shakespeare
by B.D. Barnacle

The Poetry of Landscape in Thomas Hardy
by Jeremy Mark Robinson

D.H. Lawrence: Infinite Sensual Violence
by M.K. Pace

D.H. Lawrence: Symbolic Landscapes
by Jane Foster

The Passion of D.H. Lawrence
by Jeremy Mark Robinson

Samuel Beckett Goes Into the Silence
by Jeremy Mark Robinson

RAMPOLI

RAMPOLLI

POEMS FROM MAINLY GERMAN

GEORGE MACDONALD

Edited by Carol Appleby

CRESCENT MOON

CRESCENT MOON PUBLISHING
P.O. Box 1312, Maidstone
Kent, ME14 5XU
Great Britain
www.crmoon.com

First published 2017.
© Carol Appleby 2017.

Printed and bound in the U.S.A.
Set in Bodoni Book 11 on 14pt.
Designed by Radiance Graphics.

British Library Cataloguing in Publication data available

ISBN-13 9781861715784

CONTENTS

❖

A NOTE ON THE TEXT

The text is from *Rampoli: Growths from a Long-planted Root* (1897), edited by Julian Hawthorne, and published by xx.

The last two chapters titled *Luther's Song Book* and *A Year's Diary of an Old Soul* have been omitted.

George Macdonald

George Macdonald, c. 1870, by Jeffrey of London

PREFACE TO THE TRANSLATIONS

I think every man who can should help his people to inherit the earth by bringing into his own of the wealth of other tongues. In the flower-pots of translation I offer these few exotics, with no little labour taught to exist, I hope to breathe, in English air. Such labour is to me no less serious than delightful, for to do a man's work, in the process of carrying over, more injury than must be, is a serious wrong.

I have endeavoured, first of all, to give the spirit of the poetry.

Next, I have sought to retain each individual meaning that goes to form the matter of a poem.

Third, I have aimed at preserving the peculiar mode, the aroma of the poet's style, so far as I could do it without offence to the translating English.

Fourth, both rhythm and rime being essential elements of every poem in which they are used, I have sought to respect them rigorously.

Fifth, spirit, matter, and form truly represented, the more literal the translation the more satisfactory will be the result.

After all, translation is but a continuous effort after the impossible. There is in it a general difficulty whose root has a thousand ramifications, the whole affair being but an accommodation of difficulties, and a perfect translation from one language into another is a thing that cannot be effected. One is tempted even to say that in the whole range of speech there is no such thing as a synonym.

Much difficulty arises from the comparative paucity in English of double, or feminine rimes. But I can remember only one case in which, yielding to impossibility, I have sacrificed the feminine rime: where one thing or another must go, the less valuable must be the victom.

But sometimes a whole passage has had to suffer that a specially poetic line might retain its character.

With regard to the *Hymns to the Night* and the *Spiritual Songs* of Friedrich von Hardenberg, commonly called Novalis, it is desirable to mention that they were written when the shadow of the death of his betrothed had begun to thin before the approaching dawn of his own new life. He died in 1801, at the age of twentynine. His parents belonged to the sect called Moravians, but he had become a Roman Catholic.

In the few poems from the Italian, I have found the representation of the feminine rimes, so frequent in that language, an impossibility.

NOVALIS

HYMNS TO THE NIGHT

1

Before all the wondrous shows of the widespread space around him, what living, sentient thing loves not the all-joyous light, with its colors, its rays and undulations, its gentle omnipresence in the form of the wakening Day? The giant-world of the unresting constellations inhales it as the innermost soul of life, and floats dancing in its azure flood; the sparkling, ever-tranquil stone, the thoughtful, imbibing plant, and the wild, burning multiform beast inhales it; but more than all, the lordly stranger with the sense-filled eyes, the swaying walk, and the sweetly closed, melodious lips. Like a king over earthly nature, it rouses every force to countless transformations, binds and unbinds innumerable alliances, hangs its heavenly form around every earthly substance. Its presence alone reveals the marvelous splendor of the kingdoms of the world.

Aside I turn to the holy, unspeakable, mysterious Night. Afar lies the world, sunk in a deep grave; waste and lonely is its place. In the chords of the bosom blows a deep sadness. I am ready to sink away in drops of dew, and mingle with the ashes. – The distances of memory, the wishes of youth, the dreams of childhood, the brief joys and vain hopes of a whole long life, arise in gray garments, like an evening vapor after the sunset. In other regions the light has pitched its joyous tents. What if it should never return to its children, who wait for it with the faith of innocence?

What springs up all at once so sweetly boding in my heart, and stills the soft air of sadness? Dost thou also take a pleasure in us, dark Night? What holdest thou under thy mantle, that with hidden power affects my soul? Precious balm drips from thy hand out of its bundle of poppies. Thou upliftest the heavy-laden wings of the soul.

Darkly and inexpressibly are we moved: joy-startled, I see a grave face that, tender and worshipful, inclines toward me, and, amid manifold entangled locks, reveals the youthful loveliness of the Mother. How poor and childish a thing seems to me now the Light! how joyous and welcome the departure of the day! – Didst thou not only therefore, because the Night turns away from thee thy servants, you now strew in the gulfs of space those flashing globes, to proclaim, in seasons of thy absence, thy omnipotence, and thy return?

More heavenly than those glittering stars we hold the eternal eyes which the Night hath opened within us. Farther they see than the palest of those countless hosts. Needing no aid from the light, they penetrate the depths of a loving soul that fills a loftier region with bliss ineffable. Glory to the queen of the world, to the great prophet of the holier worlds, to the guardian of blissful love! she sends thee to me, thou tenderly beloved, the gracious sun of the Night. Now am I awake, for now am I thine and mine. Thou hast made me know the Night, and brought her to me to be my life; thou hast made of me a man. Consume my body with the ardour of my soul, that I, turned to finer air, may mingle more closely with thee, and then our bridal night endure for ever.

Must the morning always return? Will the despotism of the earthly never cease? Unholy activity consumes the angel-visit of the Night. Will the time never come when Love's hidden sacrifice shall burn eternally? To the Light a season was set; but everlasting and boundless is the dominion of the Night. Endless is the duration of sleep. Holy Sleep, gladden not too seldom in this earthly day-labor, the devoted servant of the Night. Fools alone mistake thee, knowing nought of sleep but the shadow which, in the twilight of the real Night, thou pitifully castest over us. They feel thee not in the golden flood of the grapes, in the magic oil of the almond tree, and the brown juice of the poppy. They know not that it is thou who hauntest the bosom of the tender maiden, and makest a heaven of her lap; never suspect it is thou, opening the doors to Heaven, that steppest to meet them out of ancient stories, bearing the key to the dwellings of the blessed, silent messenger of secrets infinite.

3

Once when I was shedding bitter tears, when, dissolved in pain, my hope was melting away, and I stood alone by the barren mound which in its narrow dark bosom hid the vanished form of my Life, lonely as never yet was lonely man, driven by anxiety unspeakable, powerless, and no longer anything but a conscious misery; – as there I looked about me for help, unable to go on or to turn back, and clung to the fleeting, extinguished life with an endless longing: then, out of the blue distances – from the hills of my ancient bliss, came a shiver of twilight – and at once snapt the bond of birth, the chains of the Light. Away fled the glory of the world, and with it my mourning; the sadness flowed together into a new, unfathomable world. Thou, soul of the Night, heavenly Slumber, didst come upon me; the region gently upheaved itself; over it hovered my unbound, newborn spirit. The mound became a cloud of dust, and through the cloud I saw the glorified face of my beloved. In her eyes eternity reposed. I laid hold of her hands, and the tears became a sparkling bond that could not be broken. Into the distance swept by, like a tempest, thousands of years. On her neck I welcomed the new life with ecstatic tears. Never was was such another dream; then first and ever since I hold fast an eternal, unchangeable faith in the heaven of the Night, and its Light, the Beloved.

4

Now I know when will come the last morning: when the Light no more scares away the Night and Love, when sleep shall be without waking, and but one continuous dream. I feel in me a celestial exhaustion. Long and weariful was my pilgrimage to the holy grave, and crushing was the cross. The crystal wave, which, imperceptible to the ordinary sense, springs in the dark bosom of the mound against whose foot breaks the flood of the world, he who has tasted it, he who has stood on the mountain frontier of the world, and looked across into the new land, into the abode of the Night, verily he turns not again into the tumult of the world, into the land where dwells the Light in ceaseless unrest. On those heights he builds for himself tabernacles – tabernacles of peace; there longs and loves and gazes across, until the welcomest of all hours draws him down into the waters of the spring. Afloat above remains what is earthly, and is swept back in storms; but what became holy by the touch of Love, runs free through hidden ways to the region beyond, where, like odours, it mingles with love asleep. Still wakest thou, cheerful Light, that weary man to his labour, and into me pourest gladsome life; but thou wilest me not away from Memory's moss-grown monument. Gladly will I stir busy hands, everywhere behold where thou hast need of me; bepraise the rich pomp of thy splendor; pursue unwearied the lovely harmonies of thy skilled handicraft; gladly contemplate the clever pace of thy mighty, radiant clock; explore the balance of the forces and the laws of the wondrous play of countless worlds and their seasons; but true to the Night remains my secret heart, and to creative Love, her daughter. Canst *thou* show me a heart eternally true? Has thy sun friendly eyes that know me? Do thy stars lay hold of my longing hand? Do they return me the tender pressure and the caressing word? Was it thou did bedeck them with colours and a flickering outline? Or was it *she* who gave to thy jewels a higher, a dearer significance? What delight, what pleasure offers *thy* life, to outweigh the transports of Death? Wears not everything that inspirits us the livery of the Night? Thy mother, it is she brings thee forth, and to her thou owest all thy glory. Thou wouldst vanish into thyself, thou wouldst dissipate in boundless space, if she did not hold thee fast, if she swaddled thee not, so that thou grewest warm, and flaming, gavest birth to the universe. Verily I was before thou wast; the mother sent me with sisters to inhabit thy world, to sanctify it with love that it might be an ever-present memorial, to plant it with flowers unfading. As yet they have not ripened, these thoughts divine; as yet is there small trace of our coming apocalypse. One day thy clock will point to the end of Time, and then thou shalt be as one of us, and shalt, full of ardent longing, be extinguished and die. I feel in me the close of thy activity, I taste heavenly freedom, and happy restoration. With wild pangs I recognize thy distance from our home, thy feud with the ancient, glorious Heaven. Thy rage and thy raving are in vain. Inconsumable stands the cross, victory-flag of our race.

Over I pilgrim
Where every pain
Zest only of pleasure
Shall one day remain.
Yet a few moments
Then free am I,
And intoxicated
In Love's lap lie.
Life everlasting
Lifts, wave-like, at me:
I gaze from its summit
Down after thee.
Oh Sun, thou must vanish
Yon yon hillock beneath;
A shadow will bring thee
Thy cooling wreath.
Oh draw at my heart, love,
Draw till I'm gone,
That, fallen asleep, I
Still may love on.
I feel the flow of
Death's youth-giving flood;
To balsam and æther, it
Changes my blood!
I live all the daytime
In faith and in might:
And in holy rapture
I die every night.

5

In ancient times an iron Fate lorded it, with dumb force, over the
widespread families of men. A gloomy oppression swathed their
anxious souls: the earth was boundless, the abode of the gods and
their home. From eternal ages stood its mysterious structure. Beyond
the red hills of the morning, in the sacred bosom of the sea, dwelt the
sun, the all-enkindling, live luminary. An aged giant upbore the
happy world. Prisoned beneath mountains lay the first-born sons of
mother Earth, helpless in their destroying fury against the new,
glorious race of gods, and their kindred, glad-hearted men. Ocean's
dusky, green abyss was the lap of a goddess. In the crystal grottos
revelled a wanton folk. Rivers, trees, flowers, and beasts had human
wits. Sweeter tasted the wine, poured out by Youth impersonated; a
god was in the grape-clusters; a loving, motherly goddess upgrew in
the full golden sheaves; love's sacred carousal was a sweet worship of
the fairest of the goddesses. Life revelled through the centuries like
one spring-time, an ever-variegated festival of the children of and the
dewllers on the earth. All races childlike adored the ethereal,
thousand-fold flame as the one sublimest thing in the world.

It was but a fancy, a horrible dream-shape —
That fearsome to the merry tables strode,
And wrapt the spirit in wild consternation.
The gods themselves here counsel knew nor showed
To fill the stifling heart with consolation.
Mysterious was the monster's pathless road,
Whose rage would heed no prayer and no oblation;
'Twas Death who broke the banquet up with fears,
With anguish, with dire pain, and bitter tears.
Eternally from all things here disparted
That sway the heart with pleasure's joyous flow,
Divided from the loved, whom, broken-hearted,
Vain longing tosses and unceasing woe —
In a dull dream to struggle, faint and thwarted,
Seemed all was granted to the dead below!
Broke lay the merry wave of human glory
On Death's inevitable promontory.
With daring flight, aloft Thoughts pinions sweep;,
The horrid thing with beauty'ss robe men cover:
A gentle youth puts out his torch, to sleep;
Sweet comes the end, like moaning lute of lover.
Cool shadow-floods o'er melting memory creep:
So sang the song, for Misery was the mover.
Still undeciphered lay the endless Night —
The solemn symbol of a far-off Might.

The old world began to decline. The pleasure-garden of the young race withered away; up into opener, regions and desolate, forsaking his childhood, struggled the growing man. The gods vanished with their retinue. Nature stood alone and lifeless. Dry Number and rigid Measure bound her with iron chains. As into dust and air the priceless blossoms of life fell away in words obscure. Gone was wonder-working Faith, and its all-transforming, all-uniting angel-comrade, the Imagination. A cold north wind blew unkindly over the torpid plain, and the wonderland first froze, then evaporated into æther. The far depths of heaven filled with flashing worlds. Into the deeper sanctuary, into the more exalted region of the mind, the soul of the world retired with all her powers, there to rule until the dawn should break of the glory universal. No longer was the Light the abode of the gods, and the heavenly token of their presence: they cast over them the veil of the Night. The Night became the mighty womb of revelations; into it the gods went back, and fell asleep, to go abroad in new and more glorious shapes over the transfigured world. Among the people which, untimely ripe, was become of all the most scornful and insolently hostile to the blessed innocence of youth, appeared the New World, in guise never seen before, in the song-favouring hut of poverty, a son of the first maid and mother, the eternal fruit of mysterious embrace. The foreseeing, rich-blossoming wisdom of the East at once recognized the beginning of the new age; a star showed it the way to the lowly cradle of the king. In the name of the far-reaching future, they did him homage with lustre and odour, the highest wonders of Nature. In solitude the heavenly heart unfolded itelf to a flower-chalice of almighty love, upturned to the supreme face of the father, and resting on the bliss-boding bosom of the sweetly solemn mother. With deifying fervour the prophetic eye of the blooming child beheld the years to come, foresaw, untroubled over the earthly lot of his own days, the beloved offspring of his divine stem. Ere long the most childlike souls, by true love marvellously possessed, gathered about him. Like flowers sprang up a strange new life in his presence. Words inexhaustible and the most joyful fell like sparks of a divine spirit from his friendly lips. From a far shore, came a singer, born under the clear sky of Hellas, to Palestine, and gave up his whole heart to the marvellous child:-

The youth thou art who ages long hast stood
Upon our graves, lost in am aze of weening;
Sign in the darkness of God's tidings good,
Whence hints og growth humanity is gleaning;
For that we long, on that we sweetly brood
Which erst in woe had lost all life and meaning;
In everlasting life death found its goal,
For thou art Death who at last mak'st us whole.

Filled with joy, the singer went on to Indostan, his heart intoxicated with the sweetest love, and poured it out in fiery songs under that tender sky, so that a thousand hearts bowed to him, and the good news sprang up with a thousand branches. Soon after the singer's departure, his precious life was made a sacrifice for the deep fall of man. He died in his youth, torn away from his loved world, from his weeping mother, and his trembling friends. His lovely mouth emptied the dark cup of unspeakable wrongs. In horrible anguish the birth of the new world drew near. Hard he wrestled with the terrors of old Death; heavy lay the weight of the old world upon him. Yet once more he looked kindly at his mother; then came the releasing hand of the Love eternal, and he fell asleep. Only a few days hung a deep veil over the roaring sea, over the quaking land; countless tears wept his loved ones; the mystery was unsealed: heavenly spirits heaved the ancient stone from the gloomy grave. Angels sat by the sleeper, sweetly outbodied from his dreams; awaked in new Godlike glory, he clomb the limits of the new-born world, buried with his own hand the old corpse in the forsaken cavity, and with hand almighty laid upon it the stone which no power shall again upheave.

Yet weep thy loved ones over thy grave tears of joy, tears of emotion, tears of endless thanksgiving; ever afresh with joyous start, they see thee rise again, and themselves with thee; behold thee weep with soft fervour on the blessed bosom of thy mother, walk in thoughtful communion with thy friends, uttering words plucked as from the tree of life; see thee hasten, full of longing, into thy father's arms, bearing with thee youthful Humanity, and the inexhaustible cup of the golden Future. Soon the mother hastened after thee in heavenly triumph; she was the first with thee in the new home. Since then, long ages have flowed past, and in splendour ever-increasing have bestirred thy new creation, and thousands have, out of pangs and tortures, followed thee, filled with faith and longing and truth, and are walking about with thee and the heavenly virgin in the kingdom of Love, minister in the temple of heavenly Death, and forever thine.

Uplifted is the stone,
And all mankind is risen;
We all remain thine own.
And vanished is our prison.
All troubles flee away
Before thy golden cup;
For Earth nor Life can stay
When with our Lord we sup.
To the marriage Death doth call;
No virgin holdeth back;
The lamps burn lustrous all;
Of oil there is no lack.
Would thy far feet were waking
The echoes of our street!
And that the stars were making
Signal with voices sweet.
To thee, O mother maiden
Ten thousand hearts aspire;
In this life, sorrow-laden,
Thee only they desire.
In thee they hope for healing;
In thee expect true rest,
When thou, their safety sealing,
Shalt clasp them to thy breast.
With disappointment burning
Who made in hell their bed,
At last from this world turning
To thee have looked and fled:
Helpful thou hast appeared
To us in many a pain:
Now to thy home we've neared,
Not to go out again!

Now at no grave are weeping
Such as do love and pray;
The gift that Love is keeping
From none is taken away.
To soothe and quiet our longing,
Night comes, and stills the smart;
Heaven's children round us thronging
Watch and ward our heart.
Courage! for life is striding
To endless life along;
The sense in love abiding,
Grows clearer and more strong.
One day the stars, down dripping,
Shall flow in golden wine:
We, of that nectar sipping,
As living stars will shine.
Free, from the tomb emerges
Love, to die never more;
Fulfilled, life heaves and surges
A sea without a shore.
All night! all blissful leisure!
One jubilating ode!
And the sun of all our pleasure
The countenance of God.

6

Longing for Death
Into the bosom of the earth!
Out of the Light's dominions!
Death's pains are but the bursting forth
Of glad departures pinions!
Swift in the narrow little boat,
Swift to the heavenly shore we float!
Blest be the everlasting Night,
And blest the endless slumber!
We are heated with the day too bright,
And withered up with cumber!
We're weary of that life abroad:
Come, we will now go home to God!
Why longer in this world abide?
Why love and truth here cherish?
That which is old is set aside –
For us the new may perish!
Alone he stands and sore downcast
Who loves with pious warmth the Past.
The Past where yet the human spirit
In lofty flames did rise;
Where men the Father did inherit,
His countenance recognize;
And, in simplicity made ripe,
Many grew like their archetype.
The Past wherein, still rich in bloom
Old stems did burgeon glorious;
And children, for the world to come,
Sought pain and death victorious;
And, through both life and pleasure spake,
Yet many a heart for love did break.

The Past, where to the flow of youth
God yet himself declared;
And early death in loving truth
The young beheld, and dared –
Anguish and torture parient bore
To prove they loved him as of yore
With anxious yearning now we see
That Past in darkness drenched;
With this world's water never we
Shall find our hot thirst quenched:
To our old home we have to go
That blessed time again to know.
What yet doth hinder our return?
Long since repose our precious!
Their grave is of our life the bourne;
We shrink from times ungracious!
By not a hope are we decoyed:
The heart is full; the world is void.
Infinite and mysterious,
Thrills through me a sweet trembling,
As if from far there echoed thus
A sigh, our grief resembling:
The dear ones long as well as I,
And sent to me their waiting sigh.
Down to the sweet bride, and away
To the beloved Jesus!
Courage! the evening shades grow gray,
Of all our griefs to ease us!
A dream will dash our chains apart,
And lay us on the Father's heart.

I

Without thee, what were life or being!
Without thee, what had I not grown!
From fear and anguish vainly fleeing,
I in the world had stood alone;
For all I loved could trust no shelter;
The future a dim gulf had lain;
And when my heart in tears did welter,
To whom had I poured out my pain?
Consumed in love and longing lonely
Each day had worn the night's dull face;
With hot tears I had followed only
Afar life's wildly rushing race.
No rest for me, tumultuous driven!
A hopeless sorrow by the hearth! –
Who, that had not a friend in heaven,
Could to the end hold out on earth?
But if his heart once Jesus bareth,
And I of him right sure can be,
How soon a living glory scareth
The bottomless obscurity!
Manhood in him first man attaineth;
His fate in Him transfigured glows;
On freezing Iceland India gaineth,
And round the loved one blooms and blows.
Life grows a twilight softly stealing;
The world speaks all of love and glee;
For every wound grows herb of healing,

And every heart beats full and free.
I, his ten thousand gifts receiving,
Humble like him, his knees embrace;
Sure that we share his presence living
When two are gathered in one place.
Forth, forth to all highways and hedges!
Compel the wanderers to come in;
Stretch out the hand that good will pledges,
And gladly call them to their kin.
See heaven high over earth up-dawning!
In faith we see it rise and spread:
To all with us one spirit owning –
To them with us 'tis openéd.
An ancient, heavy guilt-illusion
Haunted our hearts, a changeless doom;
Blindly we strayed in night's confusion;
Gladness and grief alike consume.
Whate'er we did, some law was broken!
Mankind appeared God's enemy;
And if we thought the heavens had spoken,
They spoke but death and misery.
The heart, of life the fountain swelling –
An evil creature lay therein;
If more light shone into our dwelling,
More unrest only did we win.
Down to the earth an iron fetter
Fast held us, trembling captive crew;
Fear of Law's sword, grim Death the whetter,
Did swallow up hope's residue.
Then came a saviour to deliver –
A Son of Man, in love and might!
A holy fire, of life all-giver,
He in our hearts has fanned alight.
Then first heaven opened – and, no fable,
Our own old fatherland we trod!

To hope and trust we straight were able,
And knew ourselves akin to God.
Then vanished Sin's old spectre dismal;
Our every step grew glad and brave.
Best natal gift, in rite baptismal,
Their own faith men their children gave.
Holy in him, Life since hath floated,
A happy dream, through every heart;
We, to his love and joy devoted,
Scarce know the moment we depart.
Still standeth, in his wondrous glory,
The holy loved one with his own;
His crown of thorns, his faithful story
Still move our hearts, still make us groan.
Whoso from deadly sleep will waken,
And grasp his hand of sacrifice,
Into his heart with us is taken,
To ripen a fruit of Paradise.

II

Dawn, far eastward, on the mountain!
Gray old times are growing young:
From the flashing colour-fountain
I will quaff it deep and long! –
Granted boon to Longing's long privation!
Sweet love in divine transfiguration!
Comes at last, our old Earth's native,
All-Heaven's one child, simple, kind!
Blows again, in song creative,
Round the earth a living wind;
Blows to clear new flames that rush together
Sparks extinguished long by earthly weather.
Everywhere, from graves upspringing,
Rises new-born life, new blood!
Endless peace up to us bringing,
Dives he underneath life's flood;
Stands in midst, with full hands, eyes caressing –
Hardly waits the prayer to grant the blessing.
Let his mild looks of invading
Deep into thy spirit go;
By his blessedness unfading
Thou thy heart possessed shalt know.
Hearts of all men, spirits all, and senses
Mingle, and a new glad dance commences.
Grasp his hands with boldness yearning;
Stamp his face thy heart upon;
Turning toward him, ever turning,
Thou, the flower, must face thy sun.
Who to him his heart's last fold unfoldeth,
True as wife's his heart for ever holdeth.
Ours is now that Godhead's splendour

At whose name we used to quake!
South and north, its breathings tender,
Heavenly germs at once awake!
Let us then in God's full garden labour,
And to every bud and bloom be neighbour!

III

Who in his chamber sitteth lonely,
And weepeth heavy, bitter tears;
To whom in doleful colours, only
Of want and woe, the world appears;
Who of the Past, gulf-like receding,
Would search with questing eyes the core,
Down into which a sweet woe, pleading,
Wiles him from all sides evermore –
As if a treasure past believing
Lay there below, for him high-piled,
After whose lock, with bosom heaving,
He breathless grasps in longing wild:
He sees the Future, waste and arid,
In hideous length before him stretch;
About he roams, alone and harried,
And seeks himself, poor restless wretch! –
I fall upon his bosom, tearful:
I once, like thee, with woe was wan;
But I grew well, am strong and cheerful,
And know the eternal rest of man.
Thou too must find the one consoler
Who inly loved, endured, and died –
Even for them that wrought his dolour
With thousand-fold rejoicing died.
He died – and yet, fresh each tomorrow,
His love and him thy heart doth hold;
Thou mayst, consoled for every sorrow,
Him in thy arms with ardour fold.
New blood shall from his heart be driven
Through thy dead bones like living wine;
And once thy heart to him is given,

Then is his heart for ever thine.
What thou didst lose, he keeps it for thee;
With him thy lost love thou shalt find;
And what his hand doth once restore thee,
That hand to thee will changeless bind.

IV

Of the thousand hours me meeting,
And with gladsome promise greeting,
One alone hath kept its faith –
One wherein – ah, sorely grieved! –
In my heart I first perceived
Who for us did die the death.
All to dust my world was beaten;
As a worm had through them eaten
Withered in me bud and flower;
All my life had sought or cherished
In the grave had sunk and perished;
Pain sat in my ruined bower.
While I thus, in silence sighing,
Ever wept, on Death still crying,
Still to sad delusions tied,
All at once the night was cloven,
From my grave the stone was hoven,
And my inner doors thrown wide.
Whom I saw, and who the other,
Ask me not, or friend or brother! –
Sight seen once, and evermore!
Lone in all life's eves and morrows,
This hour only, like my sorrows,
Ever shines my eyes before.

V

If I him but have,[1]
If he be but mine,
If my heart, hence to the grave,
Ne'er forgets his love divine –
Know I nought of sadness,
Feel I nought but worship, love, and gladness.
If I him but have,
Pleased from all I part;
Follow, on my pilgrim staff,
None but him, with honest heart;
Leave the rest, nought saying,
On broad, bright, and crowded highways straying.
If I him but have,
Glad to sleep I sink;
From his heart the flood he gave
Shall to mine be food and drink;
And, with sweet compelling,
Mine shall soften, deep throughout it welling.
If I him but have,
Mine the world I hail;
Happy, like a cherub grave
Holding back the Virgin's veil:
I, deep sunk in gazing,
Hear no more the Earth or its poor praising.
Where I have but him
Is my fatherland;
Every gift a precious gem
Come to me from his own hand!
Brothers long deploréd,
Lo, in his disciples, all restoréd!

1 Here I found the double or feminine rhyme impossible without the loss of the far more precious simplicity of the original, which could be retained only by a literal translation.

VI

My faith to thee I break not,
If all should faithless be,
That gratitude forsake not
The world eternally.
For my sake Death did sting thee
With anguish keen and sore;
Therefore with joy I bring thee
This heart for evermore.
Oft weep I like a river
That thou art dead, and yet
So many of thine thee, Giver
Of life, life-long forget!
By love alone possesséd,
Such great things thou hast done!
But thou art dead, O Blessed,
And no one thinks thereon!
Thou stand'st with love unshaken
Ever by every man;
And if by all forsaken,
Art still the faithful one.
Such love must win the wrestle;
At last thy love they'll see,
Weep bitterly, and nestle
Like children to thy knee.
Thou with thy love hast found me!
O do not let me go!
Keep me where thou hast bound me
Till one with thee I grow.
My brothers yet will waken,
One look to heaven will dart –
Then sink down, love-o'ertaken,
And fall upon thy heart.

VII

HYMN

Few understand
The mystery of Love,
Know insatiableness,
And thirst eternal.
Of the Last Supper
The divine meaning
Is to the earthly senses a riddle;
But he that ever
From warm, beloved lips,
Drew breath of life;
In whom the holy glow
Ever melted the heart in trembling waves;
Whose eye ever opened so
As to fathom
The bottomless deeps of heaven –
Will eat of his body
And drink of his blood
Everlastingly.
Who of the earthly body
Has divined the lofty sense?
Who can say
That he understands the blood?
One day all is body,
One body:
In heavenly blood
Swims the blissful two.
Oh that the ocean
Were even now flushing!
And in odorous flesh

The rock were upswelling!
Never endeth the sweet repast;
Never doth Love satisfy itself;
Never close enough, never enough its own,
Can it *have* the beloved!
By ever tenderer lips
Transformed, the Partaken
Goes deeper, grows nearer.
Pleasure more ardent
Thrills through the soul;
Thirstier and hungrier
Becomes the heart;
And so endureth Love's delight
From everlasting to everlasting.
Had the refraining
Tasted but once,
All had they left
To set themselves down with us
To the table of longing
Which will never be bare;
Then had they known Love's
Infinite fullness,
And commended the sustenance
Of body and blood.

VIII

Weep I must – my heart runs over:
Would he once himself discover –
If but once, from far away!
Holy sorrow! still prevailing
Is my weeping, is my wailing:
Would that I were turned to clay!
Evermore I hear him crying
To his Father, see him dying:
Will this heart for ever beat!
Will my eyes in death close never?
Weeping all into a river
Were a bliss for me too sweet!
Hear I none but me bewailing?
Dies his name an echo failing?
Is the world at once struck dead?
Shall I from his eyes, ah! never
More drink love and life for ever?
Is he now for always dead?
Dead? What means that sound of dolour?
Tell me, tell me thou, a scholar,
What it means, that word so grim.
He is silent; all turn from me!
No one on the earth will show me
Where my heart may look for him!
Earth no more, whate'er befall me,
Can to any gladness call me!
She is but one dream of woe!
I too am with him departed:
Would I lay with him, still-hearted,
In the region down below!
Hear, me, hear, his and my father!

My dead bones, I pray thee, gather
Unto his – and soon, I pray!
Grass his hillock soon will cover,
Soon the wind will wander over,
Soon his form will fade away.
If his love they once perceived,
Soon, soon all men had believed,
Letting all things else go by!
Lord of love him only owning,
All would weep with me bemoaning,
And in bitter woe would die!

IX

He lives! he's risen from the dead!
To every man I shout:
His presence over us is spread,
Goes with us in and out.
To each I say it; each apace
His comrades telleth too –
That straight will dawn in every place
The heavenly kingdom new.
Now, to the new mind, first appears
The world a fatherland;
A new life men receive, with tears
Of rapture, from his hand.
Down into deepest gulfs of sea
Grim Death hath sunk away;
And now each man with holy glee,
Can face his coming day.
The darksome road that he hath gone
Leads out on heaven's floor;
Who heeds the counsel of the Son
Enters the Father's door.
Down here weeps no one any more
For friend that shuts his eyes;
For, soon or late, the parting sore
Will change to glad surprise.
And now to every friendly deed
Each heart will warmer glow;
For many a fold the fresh-sown seed
In lovelier fields will blow.
He lives – will sit beside our hearths,
The greatest with the least;
Therefore this day shall be our Earth's
Glad Renovation-feast.

X

The times are all so wretched!
The heart so full of cares!
The future, far outstretched,
A spectral horror wears.
Wild terrors creep and hover
With foot so ghastly soft!
Our souls black midnights cover
With mountains piled aloft.
Firm props like reeds are waving;
For trust is left no stay;
Our thoughts, like whirlpool raving,
No more the will obey!
Frenzy, with eye resistless,
Decoys from Truth's defence;
Life's pulse is flagging listless,
And dull is every sense.
Who hath the cross upheavéd
To shelter every soul?
Who lives, on high receivéd,
To make the wounded whole?
Go to the tree of wonder;
Give silent longing room:
Issuing flames asunder
Thy bad dream will consume.
Draws thee an angel tender
In saftey to the strand:
Lo, at thy feet in splendour
Lies spread the Promised Land!

XI

I know not what were left to draw me,
Had I but him who is my bliss;
If still his eye with pleasure saw me,
And, dwelling with me, me would miss.
So many search, round all ways going,
With face distorted, anxious eye,
Who call themselves the wise and knowing,
Yet ever pass this treasure by!
One man believes that he has found it,
And what he has is nought but gold;
One takes the world by sailing round it:
The deed recorded, all is told!
One man runs well to gain the laurel;
Another, in Victory's fane a niche:
By different Shows in bright apparel
All are befooled, not one made rich!
Hath He not then to you appearéd?
Have ye forgot Him turning wan
Whose side for love of us was spearéd –
The scorned, rejected Son of Man?
Of Him have you not read the story –
Heard one poor word upon the wind?
What heavenly goodness was his glory,
Or what a gift he left behind?
How he descended from the Father,
Of loveliest mother infant grand?
What Word the nations from him gather?
How many bless his healing hand?
How, thereto urged by mere love, wholly
He gave himself to us away,
And down in earth, foundation lowly,

First stone of God's new city, lay?
Can such news fail to touch us mortals?
Is not to know the man pure bliss?
Will you not open all your portals
To him who closed for you the abyss?
Will you not let the world go faring?
For Him your dearest wish deny?
To him alone your heart keep baring,
Who you has shown such favour high?
Hero of love, oh, take me, take me!
Thou art my life! my world! my gold!
Should every earthly thing forsake me,
I know who will me scatheless hold!
I see Thee my lost loves restoring!
True evermore to me thou art!
Low at thy feet heaven sinks adoring,
And yet thou dwellest in my heart!

XII

Earth's Consolation, why so slow?
Thy inn is ready long ago;
Each lifts to thee his hungering eyes,
And open to thy blessing lies.
O Father, pour him forth with might;
Out of thine arms, oh yield him quite!
Shyness alone, sweet shame, I know,
Kept him from coming long ago!
Haste him from thine into our arm
To take him with thy breath yet warm;
Thick clouds around the baby wrap,
And let him down into our lap.
In the cool streams send him to us;
In flames let him glow tremulous;
In air and oil, in sound and dew,
Let him pierce all Earth's structure through.
So shall the holy fight be fought,
So come the rage of hell to nought;
And, ever blooming, dawn again
The ancient Paradise of men.
Earth stirs once more, grows green and live;
Full of the Spirit, all things strive
To clasp with love the Saviour-guest,
And offer him the mother-breast.
Winter gives way; a year new-born
Stands at the manger's altar-horn;
'Tis the first year of that new Earth
Claimed by the child in right of birth.
Our eyes they see the Saviour well,
Yet in them doth the Saviour dwell;
With flowers his head is wreathed about;

From every flower himself smiles out.
He is the star; he is the sun;
Life's well that evermore will run;
From herb, stone, sea, and light's expanse
Glimmers his childish countenance.
His childlike labour things to mend,
His ardent love will never end;
He nestles, with unconscious art,
Divinely fast to every heart.
To us a God, to himself a child,
He loves us all, self-undefiled;
Becomes our drink, becomes our food –
His dearest thanks, a heart that's good.
The misery grows yet more and more;
A gloomy grief afflicts us sore:
Keep him no longer, Father, thus;
He will come home again with us!

XIII

When in hours of fear and failing,
All but quite our heart despairs;
When, with sickness driven to wailing,
Anguish at our bosom tears;
Then our loved ones we remember;
All their grief and trouble rue;
Clouds close in on our December
And no beam of hope shines through!
Oh but then God bends him o'er us!
Then his love comes very near!
Long we heavenward then – before us
Lo, his angel standing clear!
Life's cup fresh to us he reaches;
Whispers comfort, courage new;
Nor in vain our prayer beseeches
Rest for our beloved ones too.

XIV

Who once hath seen thee, Mother fair,
Destruction him shall never snare;
His fear is, from thee to be parted;
He loves thee evermore, true-hearted;
Thy grace remembered is the source
Whereout springs hence his spirit's highest force.
My heart is very true to thee;
My ever failing thou dost see:
Let me, sweet mother, yet essay thee –
Give me one happy sign, I pray thee.
My whole existence rests in thee:
One moment, only one, be thou with me.
I used to see thee in my dreams,
So fair, so full of tenderest beams!
The little God in thine arms lying
Took pity on his playmate crying:
But thou with high look me didst awe,
And into clouds of glory didst withdraw.
What have I done to thee, poor wretch?
To thee my longing arms I stretch!
Are not thy holy chapels ever
My resting-spots in life's endeavour?
O Queen, of saints and angels blest,
This heart and life take up into thy rest!
Thou know'st that I, beloved Queen,
All thine and only thine have been!
Have I not now, years of long measure,
In silence learned thy grace to treasure?
While to myself yet scarce confest,
Even then I drew milk from thy holy breast.
Oh, countless times thou stood'st by me!

I, merry child, looked up to thee!
His hands thy little infant gave me
In sign that one day he would save me;
Thou smiledst, full of tenderness,
And then didst kiss me: oh the heavenly bliss!
Afar stands now that gladness brief;
Long have I companied with grief;
Restless I stray outside the garden!
Have I then sinned beyond thy pardon?
Childlike thy garment's hem I pull:
Oh wake me from this dream so weariful!
If only children see thy face,
And, confident, may trust thy grace,
From age's bonds, oh, me deliver,
And make me thine own child for ever!
The love and truth of childhood's prime
Dwell in me yet from that same golden time.

XV

In countless pictures I behold thee,
O Mary, lovelily expressed,
But of them all none can unfold thee
As I have seen thee in my breast!
I only know the world's loud splendour
Since then is like a dream o'erblown;
And that a heaven, for words too tender,
My quieted spirit fills alone.

THE DISCIPLES AT SAIS

A PARABLE

Long ago, there lived far to the west a very young man, good, but extremely odd. He tormented himself continually about this nothing and that nothing, always walked in silence and straight before him, sat down alone when the others were at their sports and merry-makings, and brooded over strange things. Caves and woods were his dearest haunts; and there he talked on and on with beasts and birds, with trees and rocks – of course not one rational word, but mere idiotic stuff, to make one laugh to death. He continued, however, always moody and serious, in spite of the utmost pains that the squirrel, the monkey, the parrot, and the bullfinch could take to divert him, and set him in the right way. The goose told stories, the brook jingled a ballad between, a great thick stone cut ridiculous capers, the rose stole lovingly about him from behind and crept through his locks, while the ivy stroked his troubled brow. But his melancholy and gravity were stubborn. His parents were much troubled, and did not know what to do. He was in good health, and ate well enough; they had never caused him any offence; and, until a few years ago, he had been the liveliest and merriest of them all, foremost in all their games, and a favourite with all the maidens. He was very handsome, looked like a picture, and danced like an angel. Amongst the maidens was one, a charming and beautiful creature, who looked like wax, had hair like golden silk, and cherry-red lips, was a doll for size, and had coal-black, yes, raven-black eyes. Whoever saw her was ready to swoon, she was so lovely. Now Rosebud, for that was her name, was heartily fond of the handsome Hyacinth, for that was his name, and he loved her fit to die. The other children knew nothing of it. A violet told them of it first. The little house-cats had been quite aware of it, for the houses of their parents lay near each other. So when Hyacinth stood at night by his window, and Rosebud at hers, and the cats ran past mouse-hunting, they saw the two standing there, and often laughed and tittered so loud that they heard it and were offended. The violet told it in confidence to the strawberry, and she told it to her friend, the raspberry, who never ceased rasping when Hyacinth came along; so that by and by the whole garden and wood were in the secret, and when Hyacinth went out, he heard on all sides the cry: "Little Rosy is my posy!" This vexed him; but the next moment he could not help laughing from the bottom of his heart, when the little lizard came slipping along, sat down on a warm stone, waggled his tail, and sang:

> "Little Rosebud, good and wise,
> All at once has lost her eyes:
> Taking Hyacinth for her mother,
> Round his neck her arms she flings;
> Then perceiving 'tis another –
> Starts with terror? – no, but clings –
> Think of that! – fast as before,
> Only kissing all the more!"

Alas, how soon was the grand time over! There came a man out of strange lands, who had travelled wondrous far and wide, had a long beard, deep eyes, frightful eyebrows, and a strange garment with many folds, and inwoven with curious figures. He seated himself before the house of Hyacinth's parents. Hyacinth at once became very inquisitive, and sat down beside him, and brought him bread and wine. Then parted he his white beard, and told stories deep into the night; and Hyacinth never stirred or tired of listening. This much they learned afterward, that he talked a great deal about strange lands, unknown countries, and amazingly wonderful things; stopped there three days, and crept with Hyacinth down into deep shafts. Little Rosebud execrated the old sorcerer pretty thoroughly, for Hyacinth was altogether absorbed in his conversation, and paid no heed to anything else, hardly even to the swallowing of a mouthful of food. At length the man took his departure, but left with Hyacinth a little book which no man could read. Hyacinth gave him fruit, and bread, and wine to take with him, and accompanied him a long way. Then he came back sunk in thought, and thereafter took up a quite new mode of life. Rosebud was in a very sad way about him, for from that time forward he made little of her, and kept himself always to himself. But it came to pass that one day he came home, and was like one born again. He fell on his parents' neck and wept. "I must away to a foreign land!" he said: "the strange old woman in the wood has told me what I must do to get well; she has thrown the book into the fire, and has made me come to you to ask your blessing. Perhaps I shall be back soon, perhaps never more. Say good-bye to Rosebud for me. I should have been glad to have a talk with her; I do not know what has come to me: I must go! When I would think to recall old times, immediately come thoughts more potent in between; my rest is gone, and my heart and love with it; and I must go find them! I would gladly tell you whither, but do not myself know; it is where dwells the mother of things, the virgin with the veil; for her my spirit is on fire. Farewell!" He tore himself from them, and went out. His parents lamented and shed tears. Rosebud kept her chamber, and wept bitterly.

Hyacinth now ran, as fast as he could, through valleys and wildernesses, over mountains and streams, toward the land of mystery. Everywhere he inquired – of men and beasts, of rocks and trees, – after the sacred goddess Isis. Many laughed, many held their peace; nowhere did he get an answer. At first he passed through a rugged wild country; mists and clouds threw themselves in his way, but he rushed on impetuously. Then he came to boundless deserts of sand – mere glowing dust; and as he went his mood changed also; the time became tedious to him, and his inward unrest abated; he grew gentler, and the stormy impulse in him passed by degrees into a mild yet powerful attraction, wherein his whole spirit was dissolved. It seemed as if many years lay behind him.

And now the country became again richer and more varied, the air soft and blue, the way smoother. Green bushes enticed him with their pleasant shadows, but he did not understand their speech; they seemed indeed not to speak, and yet they filled his heart with their green hues, and their cool, still presence. Ever higher in him waxed that same sweet longing, and ever broader and juicier grew the leaves, ever louder and more jocund the birds and beasts, balmier the fruits, darker the heavenly blue, warmer the air, and more ardent his love. The time went ever faster, as if it knew itself near the goal.

One day he met a crystal rivulet, and a multitude of flowers, coming down into a valley between dark, columnar cliffs. They greeted him friendlily, with familiar words. "Dear country-folk," said he, "where shall I find the sacred dwelling of Isis? Hereabouts it must be, and here, I guess, you are more at home than I." "We also are but passing through," replied the flowers; "a spirit-family is on its travels, and we are preparing for them their road and quarters. A little way back, however, we passed through a country where we heard her name mentioned. Only go up, where we came down, and thou wilt soon learn more." The flowers and the brook smiled as they said it, offered him a cool draught, and went on their way. Hyacinth followed their counsel, kept asking, and came at last to that dwelling he had sought so long, which lay hid among palms and other rare plants. His heart beat with an infinite longing, and the sweetest apprehension thrilled him in this abode of the eternal seasons. Amid heavenly odours he fell asleep, for Dream alone could lead him into the holy of holies. In marvellous mode Dream conducted him through endless rooms full of strange things, by means of witching sounds and changeful harmonies. All seemed to him so familiar, and yet strange with an unknown splendour; then vanished the last film of the perishable as if melted into air, and he stood before the celestial virgin. Then he lifted the thin glistening veil, and – Rosebud sank into his arms. A far-off music surrounded the mysteries of love's reunion and the outpouring of their longings, and shut out from the scene of their rapture everything alien to it.

Hyacinth lived a long time after with Rosebud and his happy parents and old playmates; and numberless grandchildren thanked the wonderful old wise woman for her counsel and her uprousing; for in those days people had as many children as they pleased.

FRIEDRICH SCHILLER

THE TRYST

That was the sound of the wicket!
That was the latch as it rose!
 No – the wind that through the thicket
 Of the poplars whirring goes.

Put on thy beauty, foliage-vaulted roof,
Her to receive: with silent welcome grace her;
Ye branches build a shadowy room, eye-proof,
With lovely night and stillness to embrace her,
Ye airs caressing, wake, nor keep aloof,
In sport and gambol turning still to face her,
As, with its load of beauty, lightly borne,
Glides in the fairy foot, and dawns my morn.

What is that rustling the hedges?
She, with her hurrying pace?
 No, a bird among the sedges,
 Startled from its hiding-place!

Quench thy sunk torch, O Day! Steal out, appear,
Dim, ghostly Night, with dumbness us entrancing!
Spread thy rose-purple veil about us here;
Weave round us twigs, the mystery enhancing:
Love's rapture flees the lurking listening ear –
Flies from the Day, so indiscreetly glancing;
Hesper alone – no tattling tell-tale he –
Far-gazing, still, her confidant may be.

That was a voice, but far distant,
Faint, like a whispering low!
 No; the swan that draws persistent

❖ 63

Through the pond his circles slow!

About mine ears harmonious breathings flow;
The fountain falls in sweetly wavering rushes;
The flower beneath the west wind's kiss bends slow;
Delight from each to every thing outgushes;
Grape-clusters beckon; peaches luring glow,
And hide half in their leaves, up-swelling luscious;
The air, which aromatic odours streak,
Drinks up the glow upon my burning cheek.

Hear I not echoing footfalls
Hither adown the pleach'd walk?
    No; the over-ripened fruit falls,
      Heavy-swollen, from off its stalk!

Day's flaming eye at last is quenchéd quite;
In gentle death its colours all are paling;
Now boldly open in the fair twilight
The cups which in his blaze had long been quailing;
Slow lifts the moon her visage calmly bright;
Into great masses molten, earth sinks failing;
From every charm the zone drops unaware,
And shrouded beauty dawns upon me bare.

Yonder I see a white shimmer –
Silky – of robe or of shawl?
    No; it is the column's glimmer
      'Gainst the clipt yews' gloomy wall!

O longing heart, no more thyself befool,
Flouted by Fancy's loveliness unreal!
The empty arm no burning heart will cool,
No shadow-joy hold place for Love's Ideal!
O bring my live love all my heart to rule!

Give me her hand to hold, my every weal!
Or but the shadow of her mantle's hem –
And straight my dreams shall live, and I in them!

And soft as, from hills rosy-golden
The dews of still gladness descend,
    So had she drawn nigh unbeholden,
    And wakened with kisses her friend.

HOPE

Men talk with their lips and dream with their soul
    Of better days hitherward pacing;
To a happy, a glorious, golden goal
    See them go running and chasing!
The world grows old and to youth returns,
But still for the Better man's bosom burns.

It is Hope leads him into life and its light;
    She haunts the little one merry;
The youth is inspired by her magic might;
    Her the graybeard cannot bury:
When he finds at the grave his ended scope,
On the grave itself he planteth Hope.

She was never begotten in Folly's brain,
    An empty illusion, to flatter;
In the Heart she cries, aloud and plain:
    We are born to something better!
And that which the inner voice doth say
The hoping spirit will not betray.

THE WORDS OF FAITH

Three words I will tell you, of meaning full:
   The lips of the many shout them;
Yet were they born of no sect or school,
   The heart only knows about them:
      That man is of everything worth bereft
      Who in those three words has no faith left:

Man is born free – and is free alway
   Even were he born in fetters!
Let not the mob's cry lead you astray,
   Or the misdeeds of frantic upsetters:
      Fear not the slave when he breaks his bands;
      Fear nothing from any free man's hands.

And *Virtue* – it is no empty sound;
   That a man can obey her, no folly;
Even if he stumble all over the ground
   He yet can follow the Holy;
      And what never wisdom of wise man knew
      A child-like spirit can simply do.

And a *God* there is – a steadfast Will,
   However the human shrinketh!
High over space and time He still,
   The live Thought, doth what He thinketh;
      And though all things keep circling, to change confined,
      He keeps, in all changes, a changeless mind.

These three words cherish – of meaning full:
   From mouth to mouth send them faring;
For, although they spring from no sect or school,

Your hearts them witness are bearing;
   And man is never of worth bereft
   While yet he has faith in those three words left.

Three words there are of weighty sound,
   And from good men's lips they hail us;
But a tinkling cymbal, a drum's rebound,
   For help or for comfort they fail us!
     His Life's fruit away he forfeit flings
     Who catches after those shadows of things;

Who still believes in a Golden Age,
   Where the Right and the Good reign in splendour:
The Right and the Good war ever must wage –
   Their foe will never surrender;
     And chok'st thou him not in the upper air,
     His strength he will still on the earth repair.

Who yet believes that Fortune, the jilt,
   To the noble will bind herself ever:
Her love-looks follow the man of guilt;
   The world to the good belongs never;
     He is in it a stranger; he wanders away
     Seeking a house that will not decay.

Who still believes that no human gaze
   Truth ever her visage discloses:
Her veil no mortal hand shall raise;
   Man only thinks and supposes:
     Thou mayst prison the spirit in sounding form,
     But the Fetterless walks away on the storm.

Then, noble spirit, from folly break free,
   This heav'nly faith holding and handing:
What the ear never heard, what no eye can see,

Is the lovely, the true, notwithstanding;
  Outside, the fool seeks for it evermore;
  The wise man finds it with closed door!

THE METAPHYSICIAN

"How far the world lies under me!
Scarce can I see the men below there crawling!
How high it bears me up, my lofty calling!
How near the heavenly canopy!"
Thus, from tower-roof where he doth clamber,
Calls out the slater; and with him the small big man,
Jack Metaphysicus, down in his writing-chamber!
Tell me, thou little great big man, –
The tower, whence thou so grandly all things hast inspected,
Of what is it? – Whereon is it erected?
How cam'st thou up thyself? Its heights so smooth and bare –
How serve they thee but thence into the vale to stare?

THE PHILOSOPHERS

The principle whence everything
  To life and shape ascended –
The pulley whereon Zeus the ring
Of Earth, which else in sherds would spring,
  Has carefully suspended –
To genius I yield him a claim
Who fathoms for me what its name,
  Save I withdraw its curtain:
  It is – ten is not thirteen.

That snow makes cold, that fire burns,
  That man on two feet goeth,
That in the heavens the sun sojourns –
This much the man who logic spurns
  Through his own senses knoweth;
But metaphysics who has got,
Knows he that burneth, freezeth not;
  Knows 'tis the moist that wetteth,
  And 'tis the rough that fretteth.

Great Homer sings his epic high;
  The hero fronts his dangers;
The brave his duty still doth ply –
And did it while, I won't deny,
  Philosophers were strangers:
But grant by heart and brain achiev'd
What Locke and Des Cartes ne'er conceiv'd –
  By them yet, as behovéd,
  It possible was provéd.

Strength for the Right is counted still;

Bold laughs the strong hyena;
Who rule not, servants' parts must fill;
It goes quite tolerably ill
   Upon this world's arena;
But how it would be, if the plan
Of the universe now first began,
   In many a moral system
   All men may read who list 'em.

"Man needs with man must linked be
   To reach the goal of growing;
In the whole only worketh he;
Many drops go to make the sea;
   Much water sets mills going.
Then with the wild wolves do not stand,
But knit the state's enduring band:"
   From doctor's chair thus, tranquil,
   Herr Pufendorf and swan-quill.

But since to all, what doctors say
   Flies not as soon as spoken,
Nature will use her mother-way,
See that her chain fly not in tway,
   The circle be not broken:
Meantime, until the world's great round
Philosophy in one hath bound,
   She keeps it on the move, sir,
   By hunger and by love, sir.

SAYINGS OF CONFUCIUS

I

Threefold is of Time the tread:
Lingering comes the Future pacing hither;
Dartlike is the Now gone thither;
Stands the Past aye moveless, foot and head.

    No impatience wings its idle
Tread of leisurely delay;
Fear or doubt it cannot bridle
Should it headlong run away;
No remorse, no incantation
Moves the standing from its station.

    Wouldst thou end thy earthly journey
Wise and of good fortune full,
Make the Lingering thine attorney
Thee to counsel – not thy tool;
Not for friend the Flying take,
Nor thy foe the Standing make.

II

Threefold is of Space the way:
    On unresting, without stay,
    Strives the Length into the distance;
    Ceaseless pours the Breadth's insistence
    Bottomless the Depth goes down.

For a sign the three are sent thee:
    Onward must alone content thee –

Weary, thou must not stand still
Wouldst thou thy perfection fill!
Thou must spread thee wider, bigger,
Wouldst thou have the world take figure!
To the deep the man descendeth
Who existence comprehendeth.
Leads persistence to the goal;
Leads abundance to precision;
Dwells in the abyss the Vision.

• • • • •

*In the following epigrams I have altered the form,
which in the original is the elegiac distich.*

KNOWLEDGE

To this man, 'tis a goddess tall,
  Who lifts a star-encircled head;
To that, a fine cow in a stall,
  Which gives him butter to his bread.

MY FAITH

Which religion I profess?
  None of which you mention make.
Wherefore so? – And can't you guess?
  For Religion's sake.

FRIEND AND FOE

Dear is my friend, but my foe too
   Is friendly to my good;
My friend the thing shows I *can* do,
   My foe, the thing I should.

EXPECTATION AND FULFILMENT

Thousand-masted, mighty float,
  Out to sea Youth's navy goes:
Silent, in his one saved boat,
  Age into the harbour rows.

THE DIVER

"Which of you, knight or squire, will dare
  Plunge into yonder gulf?
A golden beaker I fling in it – there!
  The black mouth swallows it like a wolf!
Who brings me the cup again, whoever,
It is his own – he may keep it for ever!"

Tis the king who speaks; and he flings from the brow
  Of the cliff, that, rugged and steep,
Hangs out o'er the endless sea below,
  The cup in the whirlpool's howling heap: –
"Again I ask, what hero will follow?
What brave heart plunge into yon dark hollow?"

The knights and the squires, the king about,
  Hear him, and dumbly stare
Into the wild sea's tumbling rout;
  But to win the beaker, they hardly care!
The king, for the third time, round him glaring –
"Not a soul of you has the daring?"

Speechless all, as before, they stand:
  When a vassal bold, gentle, and gay,
Steps out from his comrades' shrinking band,
  Flinging his girdle and cloak away;
And all the women and men that surrounded
Gazed on the grand-looking youth, astounded.

And when he stepped to the rock's rough brow
  Looking down on the gulf so black,
The waters which it had swallowed, now

Charybdis bellowing rendered back;
And, with a roar as of distant thunder,
Foaming they burst from the dark lap under.

It wallows, seethes, hisses, in raging rout,
   As when water wrestles with fire,
Till to heaven the yeasty tongues they spout;
   And flood upon flood keeps mounting higher:
It will never its endless coil unravel,
As the sea with another sea were in travail!

But, at last, slow sinks the writhing spasm,
   And, black through the foaming white,
Downward gapes a yawning chasm –
   Bottomless, cloven to hell's wide night;
And, sucked up, see the billows roaring
Down through the whirling funnel pouring!

Then in haste, ere the out-rage return again,
   The youth to his God doth pray,
And – ascends a cry of horror and pain –
   Already the vortex hath swept him away!
And o'er the bold swimmer, in darkness eternal,
Close the great jaws of the gulf infernal!

Then the water above grows smooth as glass,
   While, below, dull roarings ply;
And, trembling, they hear the murmur pass –
   "High-hearted youth, farewell! good-bye!"
And, hollower still, comes the howl affraying,
Till their hearts are sick with the frightful delaying.

If the crown itself thou in should fling,
   And say, "Who back with it hies
Himself shall wear it, and shall be king,"

I should not covet the precious prize!
What Ocean hides in that howling hell of it,
Live soul will never come back to tell of it!

Ships many, caught in that whirling surge,
    Shot sheer to their dismal doom:
Keel and mast only did ever emerge,
    Shattered, from out the all-gulping tomb! –
Like the bluster of tempest, clearer and clearer,
Comes its roaring nearer and ever nearer!

It wallows, seethes, hisses, in raging rout,
    As when water wrestles with fire,
Till to heaven the yeasty tongues they spout,
    Wave upon wave's back mounting higher;
And as with the rumble of distant thunder
Bellowing it bursts from the dark lap under.

And see, from its bosom, flowing dark,
    Something heave up, swan-white!
An arm and a shining neck they mark,
    And it rows with unrelaxing might!
It is he! and aloft in his left hand holden,
He swings, recovered, the beaker golden!

With long deep breaths his path he ploughed,
    Glad greeting the heavenly day;
Jubilant shouted the gazing crowd,
    "He lives! he is free! he has burst his way!
Out of the grave, the whirlpool uproarious,
The hero hath rescued his life victorious!"

He comes; they surround him with shouts of glee;
    At the king's feet he sinks on the sod,
And hands him the beaker upon his knee.

To his lovely daughter the king gives a nod:
She fills it brim-full of wine sparkling and raying;
And then to the monarch the youth turned, saying:

"Long live the king! – Ah, well doth he fare
    Who breathes in this rosy light!
For frightful, yea, horrible is it down there;
    And man ought not to tempt the heavenly Might,
Or long to see, with prying unwholesome,
What He graciously covers with darkness dolesome!

"It tore me down as on lightning's wing –
    When a shaft in a rock outpours,
Wild-rushing against me, a torrent spring:
    Its conflict seized me with raging force
And like a top, with giddy twisting,
Spun me about: there was no resisting!

"Then God did show me, sore beseeching
    In deepest, frightfullest need,
Up from the bottom a rock-ledge reaching –
    At it I caught, and from death was freed!
And behold, on spiked corals the beaker suspended
Which had else to the very abyss descended!

"For below me it lay yet mountain-deep
    The purply darksome maw!
And, though to the ear it was dead asleep,
    The ghasted eye, down staring, saw
How, with dragons, lizards, salamanders, crawling,
The hell-jaws horrible were sprawling!

"Black-swarming, in medley miscreate,
    In masses lumped hideously,
Wallowed the conger, the thorny skate,

The lobster's grisly deformity;
And, baring its teeth with cruel sheen, a
Terrible shark, the sea's hyena.

"So there I hung, and shuddering knew
  That human help was none;
One thinking soul mid the horrid crew,
  In the ghastly desert I was alone –
Deeper than human speech e'er sounded,
By the sad waste's dismal monsters surrounded!

"Thus thought I, and shivered. Then a something crept near
  Upon legs with a hundred joints!
It snaps at me suddenly: frantic with fear
  I lost my grasp of the coral points:
Away the whirl in its raging tore me –
But it was my salvation, and upward bore me!"

The king at the tale is filled with amaze: –
  "The beaker, well won, is thine;
And this ring I will give thee too," he says,
  "Precious with gems that are more than fine,
If thou dare it yet once, and bring me the story
Of what's in the sea's lowest repertory."

His daughter she hears him with tender dismay,
  And with sweet words suasive doth plead:
"Father, enough of this cruel play!
  For you he has done an unheard-of deed!
If you may not master your heart's desire,
'Tis the knights' turn now to shame the squire!"

The king sudden snatches and hurls the cup
  Into the swirling pool: –
"If thou bring me once more that beaker up,

Thou art best of my knights, the most worshipful!
And this very day to thy home thou shalt lead her
Who stands there – for thee such a pitiful pleader."

A passion divine his being invades;
   His eyes dart a lightning ray;
He sees of her blushes the changeful shades,
   He sees her grow pallid and sink away!
Determination thorough him flashes,
And downward for life or for death he dashes!

They hear the dull roar: 'tis returning again,
   Announced by the thunderous brawl!
Downward they bend with loving strain:
   They come! they are coming, the waters all! –
They rush up! – they rush down! they rush ever and ever:
The youth to the daylight rises never!

KNIGHT TOGGENBURG

True love, knight, as to a brother,
   Yield I you again;
Ask me not for any other,
   For it gives me pain.
Calmly I behold you come in,
   Calm behold you go;
Your sad eyes the weeping dumb in
   I nor read nor know.

And he hears her uncomplaining,
   Tears him free by force;
To his heart but once her straining,
   Flings him on his horse;
Sends to all his vassals merry
   In old Switzerland;
To the holy grave they hurry,
   White-crossed pilgrim band.

Mighty deeds, the foe outbraving,
   Works their hero-arm;
From their helms the plumes float waving
   Mid the heathen swarm;
Still his *"Toggenburg"* upwaking
   Frays the Mussulman;
But his heart its grievous aching
   Quiet never can.

One whole year he did endure it,
   Then his patience lost;
Peace, he never could secure it,
   And forsakes the host;

Sees a ship by Joppa's entry
    At her cable saw;
Sails him home to that dear country
    Where she breath doth draw.

At the gate, her castle under,
    Pilgrim sad, he knocked;
Straight, as with a word of thunder
    Was the gate unlocked:
"She you seek, with rites most solemn
    Is betrothed to heaven;
Yesterday, beneath that column,
    She to Christ was given."

Then the halls he leaves for ever
    Of his ancestors;
Shield or sword sets eyes on never,
    Or his faithful horse.
Down from Toggenburg he fareth,
    None to see or care;
On his noble limbs he weareth
    Sackcloth made of hair:

And himself a hovel buildeth
    That same cloister nigh,
Where the lime-tree thicket yieldeth
    Cover whence to spy.
There, from morning's earliest traces
    Till red evening shone,
Thither turned his hoping face is,
    There he sits alone.

On the walls so high above him,
    His eyes waiting hang,
Waiting, though she would not love him,

For her lattice-clang –
Waiting till the loved should send her
   Glance into the vale,
And, unthinking, toward it bend her
   Visage, angel-pale.

Then he laid him, sadness scorning,
   Comforted to sleep;
Quietly joyous till the morning
   Out again should peep.
And so sat he, years a many,
   Years without a pang,
Waiting without murmur any
   Till her window rang –

For the lovely one to send her
   Glance into the vale,
And, unseeing, toward him bend her
   Angel visage pale.
And thus sat he, staring wanly,
   His last morning there:
Toward her window still the manly
   Silent face did stare.

LONGING

Ah, from out this valley hollow,
    By cold fogs always oppressed,
Could I but the outpath follow –
    Ah, how were my spirit blest!
Hills I see there, glad dominions,
    Ever young, and green for aye!
Had I wings, oh, had I pinions,
    To the hills were I away!

Harmonies I hear there ringing,
    Tones of sweetest heavenly rest;
And the gentle winds are bringing
    Balmy odours to my breast!
Golden fruits peep out there, glowing
    Through the leaves to Zephyr's play;
And the flowers that there are blowing
    Will become no winter's prey!

Oh, what happy things are meeting
    There, in endless sunshine free!
And the airs on those hills greeting,
    How reviving must they be!
But me checks yon raving river
    That betwixt doth chafe and roll;
And its dark waves rising ever
    Strike a horror to my soul!

See a skiff on wild wave heaving!
    But no sailor walks the mole.
Quick into it, firm believing,
    For its sails they have a soul!

❖ 88

Thou must trust, nor wait to ponder:
  God will give no pledge in hand;
Nought but miracle bears yonder
  To the lovely wonderland!

JOHANN WOLFGANG VON GOETHE

POEMS

Poems are painted window-panes:
Look from the square into the church –
Gloom and dusk are all your gains!
Sir Philistine is left in the lurch:
Outside he stands – spies nothing or use of it,
And nought is left him save the abuse of it.

But you, I pray you, just step in;
Make in the chapel your obeisance:
All at once 'tis a radiant pleasaunce:
Device and story flash to presence;
A gracious splendour works to win.
This to God's children is full measure:
It edifies and gives them pleasure.

LEGEND

AFTER THE MANNER OF HANS SACHS

While yet unknown, and very low,
Our Lord on earth went to and fro;
And some of his scholars his word so good
Very strangely misunderstood –
He much preferred to hold his court
In streets and places of resort,
Because under the heaven's face
Words better and freer flow apace;
There he gave them the highest lore
Out of his holy mouth in store;
Wondrously, by parable and example,
Made every market-place a temple.

So faring, in his heart content,
Once with them to a town he went –
Saw something blinking on the way,
And there a broken horse-shoe lay!
He said thereon St. Peter to,
"Prithee now, pick up that shoe."
St. Peter was not in fitting mood:
He had been dreaming all the road
Some stuff about ruling of the world,
Round which so many brains are twirled –
For in the head it seems so easy!
And with it his thoughts were often busy;
Therefore the finding was much too mean;
Crown and sceptre it should have been!
He was not one his back to bow

After half an iron-shoe!
Therefore aside his head he bended,
And that he had not heard pretended.

In his forbearance the Lord did stoop
And lift himself the horse-shoe up;
Then for the present he did wait.
But when they reach the city-gate,
He goes up to a blacksmith's door,
Receives three pence the horse-shoe for;
And as they through the market fare,
Seeing for sale fine cherries there,
He buys of them so few or so many
As they will give for a three-penny;
Which he, thereon, after his way,
Up in his sleeve did quietly lay.

Now, from the other gate, they trod
Through fields and meads a housless road;
The path of trees was desolate,
The sun shone out, the heat was great;
So that one in a region such
For a drink of water had given much.
The Lord goes ever before them all,
And as by chance lets a cherry fall:
In a trice St. Peter was after it there
As if a golden apple it were!
Sweet to his palate was the berry.
Then by and by, another cherry
Down on the ground the Master sends,
For which St. Peter as quickly bends.
So, many a time, the Lord doth let
Him bend his back a cherry to get.
A long time thus He let him glean;
Then said the Lord, with look serene:

"If at the right time thou hadst bent,
Thou hadst found it more convenient!
Of little things who little doth make
For lesser things must trouble take."

THE CASTLE ON THE MOUNTAIN

Up there, upon yonder mountain,
  Stands a castle old, in the gorse,
Where once, behind doors and portals,
  Lurking lay knight and horse.

Burnt are the doors and the portals;
  All round it is very still;
Its old walls, tumbled in ruins,
  I scramble about at my will.

Close hereby lay a cellar
  Full of wine that was old and rare;
But the cheery maid with the pitchers
  No more comes down the stair;

No more in the hall, sedately
  Sets the beaker before the guest;
No more at the festival stately,
  The flagon fills for the priest;

No more to the page so thirsty
  Gives a draught in the corridor;
And receives for the hurried favour
  The hurried thanks no more.

For every rafter and ceiling
  Long ago were to ashes burned,
And stair and passage and chapel
  To rubbish and ruin turned.

Yet when, with flask and cittern,

On a day in the summer's prime,
Up to the rocky summit
   I watched my darling climb –

Out came the old joy reviving
   On the face of the ancient rest,
And on went the old life driving,
   In its lordliness and zest;

It seemed as for strangers distinguished
   Their state-rooms they did prepare,
And out of that brave time, shadowy
   Came stepping a youthful pair.

And the worthy priest in his chapel
   Stood already in priestly dress,
And asked – Will you two take one another?
   And smiling we answered – Yes;

And the hymns with deep pulsation
   Stirred every heart at once;
And instead of the congregation
   The echo yelled response.

And when, in the gathered evening,
   Profound the stillness grew,
And the red-glowing sun at the broken
   Gable came peering through,

Then damsel and page, in his rays, are
   Grandees of the olden prime;
She tastes of his cup at her leisure,
   And he to thank her takes time.

LUDWIG UHLAND

THE LOST CHURCH

In the far forest, overhead,
  A bell is often heard obscurely;
How long since first, no one can tell –
  Nor can report explain it surely:
From the lost church, the rumour hath,
  Out on the winds the ringing goeth;
Once full of pilgrims was the path –
  Now where to find it, no one knoweth.

Deep in the wood I lately went
  Where no foot-trodden way is lying;
From times corrupt, on evil bent,
  My heart to God went out in sighing:
There, in the wild wood's deep repose,
  I heard the ringing somewhat nearer;
The higher that my longing rose
  Its peal grew fuller and came clearer.

My thoughts upon themselves did brood;
  My sense was with the sound so busy
That I have never understood
  How I did climb that steep so dizzy.
It seemed more than a hundred years
  Had passed me over, dreaming, sighing –
When far above the clouds appears
  An open space in sunlight lying.

Dark-blue the heavens above it bowed;
  The sun was radiant, large, and glowing;
And, see, a minister's structure proud
  Stood in the rich light, golden showing.

❖ 98

The clouds around it, sunny-clear,
  Seemed bearing it aloft like pinions;
Its spire-point seemed to disappear,
  Slow vanishing in heaven's dominions.

The bell's clear tones, of rapture full,
  Boomed in the tower and made it quiver;
No mortal hand that rope did pull –
  A dumb storm made it swing and shiver.
It seemed to heave my throbbing breast,
  That heavenly storm with torrent blended:
With wavering step, yet hopeful quest,
  Into the church my way I wended.

What met me there as in I trode
  With syllables cannot be painted;
Darksome yet clear, the windows glowed
  With forms of all the martyrs sainted.
Then saw I, radiantly unfurled,
  Form swell to life and break its barriers;
I looked abroad into a world
  Of holy women and God's warriors.

Down at the alter I kneeled soft,
  With love and prayer my heart allegiant:
Upon the ceiling, far aloft,
  Was painted Heaven's resplendent pageant;
But when again I lift mine eyes,
  Lo, the high vault has flown asunder!
The upward gate wide open lies,
  And every veil unveils a wonder.

What gloriousness I then beheld
  With silent worship, speechless wonder;
What blessed sounds upon me swelled,

Like organs' and like trumpets' thunder –
　No human words could ever tell! –
But who for such is sighing sorest,
　Let him give heed unto the bell
That dimly soundeth in the forest.

THE DREAM

In a garden sweet went walking
   Two lovers hand in hand;
Two pallid figures, low talking,
   They sat in the flowery land.

They kissed on the cheek one another,
   And they kissed upon the mouth;
They held in their arms each the other,
   And back came their health and youth.

Two little bells rang shrilly –
   And the lovely dream was dead!
She lay in the cloister chilly;
   He afar on his dungeon-bed.

HEINRICH HEINE

LIEDER

IV

Thy little hand lay on my bosom, dear:
What a knocking in that little chamber! – dost hear?
There dwelleth a carpenter evil, and he
Is hard at work on a coffin for me.

He hammers and knocks by night and by day;
'Tis long since he drove all my sleep away:
Ah, haste thee, carpenter, busy keep,
That I the sooner may go to sleep!

LYRISCHES INTERMEZZO

XXXVIII

The phantoms of times forgotten
   Arise from out their grave,
And show me how once in thy presence
   I lived the life it gave.

In the day I wandered dreaming,
   Through the streets with unsteady foot;
The people looked at me in wonder,
   I was so mournful and mute.

At night, then it was better,
   For empty was the town;
I and my shadow together
   Walked speechless up and down.

My way, with echoing footstep,
   Over the bridge I took;
The moon broke out of the waters,
   And gave me a meaning look.

I stopped before thy dwelling,
   And gazed, and gazed again –
Stood staring up at thy window,
   My heart was in such pain.

I know that thou from thy window
   Didst often look downward – and
Sawest me, there in the moonlight,
   A motionless pillar stand.

LYRISCHES INTERMEZZO

XLI

I dreamt of the daughter of a king,
  With white cheeks tear-bewetted;
We sat 'neath the lime tree's leavy ring,
  In love's embraces netted.

"I would not have thy father's throne,
  His crown or his golden sceptre;
I want my lovely princess alone –
  From Fate that so long hath kept her."

"That cannot be," she said to me:
  "I lie in the grave uncheerly;
And only at night I come to thee,
  Because I love thee so dearly."

LYRISCHES INTERMEZZO

XLV

In the sunny summer morning
  Into the garden I come;
The flowers are whispering and talking,
  But for me, I wander dumb.

The flowers are whispering and talking;
  They pity my look so wan:
"Thou must not be cross with our sister,
  Thou sorrowful, pale-faced man!"

LYRISCHES INTERMEZZO

LXIV

Night lay upon mine eyelids;
  Upon my mouth lay lead;
With rigid brain and bosom,
  I lay among the dead.

How long it was I know not
  That sleep oblivion gave;
I wakened up, and, listening,
  Heard a knocking at my grave.

"Tis time to rise up, Henry!
  The eternal day draws on;
The dead are all arisen –
  The eternal joy's begun."

"My love, I cannot raise me;
  For I have lost my sight;
My eyes with bitter weeping
  They are extinguished quite."

"From thy dear eyelids, Henry,
  I'll kiss the night away;
Thou shalt behold the angels,
  And Heaven's superb display."

"My love, I cannot raise me;
  Still bleeds my bosom gored,
Where thou heart-deep didst stab me
  With a keen-pointed word."

"Soft I will lay it, Henry,
    My hand soft on thy heart;
And that will stop its bleeding
    And soothe at once the smart."

"My love, I cannot raise me –
    My head is bleeding too;
When thou wast stolen from me
    I shot it through and through!"

"I with my tresses, Henry,
    Will stop the fountain red;
Press back again the blood-stream,
    And heal thy wounded head."

She begged so sweetly, dearly,
    I could no more say no;
I tried, I strove to raise me,
    And to my darling go.

Then the wounds again burst open;
    With torrent force outbrake
From head and breast the blood-stream,
    And, lo, I came awake!

DIE HEIMKEHR

LX

They have company this evening,
   And the house is full of light;
Up there at the shining window
   Moves a shadowy form in white.

Thou seest me not – in the darkness
   I stand here below, apart;
Yet less, ah less thou seest
   Into my gloomy heart!

My gloomy heart it loves thee,
   Loves thee in every spot:
It breaks, it bleeds, it shudders – But
   Into it thou seest not!

LXII

Diamonds hast thou, and pearls,
  And all by which men lay store;
And of eyes thou hast the fairest –
  Darling, what wouldst thou more?

Upon thine eyes so lovely
  Have I a whole army-corps
Of undying songs composed –
  Dearest, what wouldst thou more?

And with thine eyes so lovely
  Thou hast tortured me very sore,
And hast ruined me altogether –
  Darling, what wouldst thou more?

THE NORTH SEA

FIRST CYCLE

XII. PEACE[2]

High in heaven the sun was glowing,
White cloud-waves were round him flowing;
The sea was still and grey.
Thinking in dreams, by the helm I lay:
Half waking, half in slumber, then
Saw I Christ, the Saviour of men.
In undulating garments white
He walked in giant shape and height
Over land and sea.
High in the heaven up towered his head;
His hands in blessing forth he spread
Over land and sea.
And for a heart, in his breast
He bore the sun; there did it rest.
The red, flaming heart of the Lord
Out its gracious radiance poured,
Its fair and love-caressing light
With illuminating and warming might
Over land and sea.

Sounds of solemn bells that go
Through the air to and fro,
Drew, like swans in rosy traces,
With soft, solemn, stately graces,

---

2 Footnote: I have here used rimes although the original has none. With notions of
translating severer now than when, many years ago, I attempted this poem, I should not
now take such a liberty. In a few other points also the translation is not quite close enough
to please me; but it must stand.

The gliding ship to the green shore –
Peopled, for many a century hoar,
By men who dwell at rest in a mighty
Far-spreading and high-towered city.

Oh, wonder of peace, how still was the town!
The hollow tumult had all gone down
Of the babbling and stifling trades;
And through each clean and echoing street
Walked men and women, and youths and maids,
White clothes wearing,
Palm branches bearing;
And ever and always when two did meet,
They gazed with eyes that plain did tell
They understood each other well;
And trembling, in self-renouncement and love,
Each a kiss on the other's forehead laid,
And looked up to the Saviour's sunheart above,
Which, in joyful atoning, its red blood rayed
Down upon all; and the people said,
From hearts with threefold gladness blest,
    Lauded be Jesus Christ!

JOHAN GAUDENZ
VON SALIS-SEEWIS

THE GRAVE

The grave is deep and soundless,
  Its brink is ghastly lone;
With veil all dark and boundless
  It hides a land unknown.

The nightingale's sweet closes
  Down there come not at all;
And friendship's withered roses
  On the mossy hillock fall.

Their hands young brides forsaken
  Wring bleeding there in vain;
The cries of orphans waken
  No answer to their pain.

Yet nowhere else for mortals
  Dwells their implored repose;
Through none but those dark portals
  Home to his rest man goes.

The poor heart, here for ever
  By storm on storm beat sore,
Its true peace gaineth never
  But where it beats no more.

PSYCHES MOURNING

Psyche moans, in deep-sunk, darksome prison,
For redemption; ah! for light she aches;
Fears, hopes, after every noise doth listen –
Whether Fate her bars of iron breaks.

Bound are Psyche's pinions – airy, soaring;
Yet high-hearted is she, groaning low;
Knows that under clouds whence rain is pouring
Sprouts the palm that crowns the victor's brow;

Knows among the thorns the rose yet reigneth;
Golden flowers spring from the desert grave
She her garland through denial gaineth,
And her strength is steeled by winds that rave.

'Tis through lack that she her blisses buyeth;
Sorrow's dream comes true by longing long;
Lest light break the sleep wherein she lieth,
Round her tree of life the shadows throng.

Psyche's wail is but a fluted sadness
Heard from willows the moon silvereth;
Psyche's tears are dews of morning redness,
And her sighs the sweet night-violet's breath!

Yews o'ershade the myrtle of her probation;
Much she loves for great has been her dole;
Love leads through the paths of separation,
Leads her to reunion's joyous goal.

She endures; bravely bears every burden,

Dumb before the will of Fate bends low;
Lies her bliss the patient tranquil word in;
Her one cordial, feeling's overflow!

Preconviction – ah! the call, the token,
Spreading wings the darksome sky to cleave!
'Tis but boding! 'tis but knowledge broken!
Truth's but what she truly doth believe!

Darkness hides the goal of Psyche's mission;
For the eyes that tears so often gall
Reach not to the summit of completion
Where illusion's vaporous veil doth fall!

MATTHIAS CLAUDIUS

THE MOTHER BY THE CRADLE

Sleep, baby boy, sleep sweet, secure;
  Thy father's very miniature!
That art thou, though thy father goes
  And says that thou hast not his nose.

This very moment here was he,
  His face o'er thine did pose
And said – Much has he sure of me,
  But no, 'tis not my nose.

I think myself, it is too small,
  But it is *his* nose after all;
For if thy nose his nose be not,
  Whence came the nose that thou hast got?

Sleep, boy! thy father only chose
  To tease me – that's his part!
Never you mind about his nose,
  But see you have his heart.

CONTENTMENT

I am content. In triumph's tone
    My song, let people know!
And many a mighty man, with throne
    And sceptre, is not so.
And if he is, why then, I cry,
The man is just the same as I.

The Mogul's gold, the Sultan's show,
    The hero's bliss, who, vext
To find no other world below,
    Up to the moon looked next –
I'd none of them; for things like that
Are only fit for laughing at.

My motto is – Content with this.
    Gold – rank – I prize not such.
That which I have, my measure is;
    Wise men desire not much.
Men wish and wish, and have their will,
And wish again, as hungry still.

And gold or honour, though it rings,
    Is but a brittle glass;
Experience of changing things
    Might teach a very ass!
Right often Many turns to None,
And honour has but a short run.

To do right, to be good and clear,
    Is more than rank and gold;
Then art thou always of good cheer,

And blisses hast untold;
Then art thou with thyself at one,
And hatest no man, fearest none.

I am content. In triumph's tone,
  My song, let people know!
And many a mighty man, with throne
  And sceptre, is not so.
And if he is, why then, I cry,
The man is just the same as I.

PETRUS AUGUSTUS DE GENESTET

THREE PAIRS AND ONE

You have two ears – and but one mouth:
   Let this, friend, be a token –
Much should be heard, and not so much
      Be spoken.

You have two eyes – and but one mouth:
   That is an indication –
Much must you see, but little serves
      Relation.

You have two hands – and but one mouth:
   Receive the hint you meet with –
For labour two, but only one
      To eat with.

ANONYMOUS

FROM THE GERMAN

SONG OF THE LONELY

Son, first-born, at home abiding!
  All without is cold and bare:
Hide me from the tempest's chiding
  Warm beside the Father's chair.

I am homesick, Lord of splendour!
  Twilight fills my soul with fright:
Let thy countenance befriend her,
  Shining from the halls of light.

I am homesick, loving Father!
  Long years hath the pain increased:
Soon, oh soon! thy children gather
  To the endless marriage-feast.

FRANCESCO PETRARCH

PART I. SONNET LIX

I am so weary with the burden old
Of foregone faults, and power of custom base,
That much I fear to perish from the ways,
And fall into my enemy's grim fold.
True, a high friend, to free me, not with gold,
Came, of ineffable and utmost grace –
Then straightway vanished from before my face,
So that in vain I strive him to behold.
But his voice yet comes echoing below:
O ye that labour, the way open lies!
Come unto me lest some one shut the gate!
– What heavenly grace – what love will – or what fate –
The pinions of a dove on me bestow
That I may rest, and from the earth arise?

PART II. SONNET LXXV

The elect angels and the souls in bliss,
The citizens of heaven, when, that first day,
My lady passed from me and went their way,
Of marvel and pity full, did round her press.
"What light is this, and what new loveliness?"
They said among them; "for such sweet display
Did never mount, that from the earth did stray
To this high dwelling, all this age, we guess!"[3]
She, well content her lodging chang'd to find,
Shows perfect, by her peers most perfect placed;
And now and then half turning looks behind
To see if I walk in the way she traced:
Hence I lift heavenward all my heart and mind
Because I hear her pray me to make haste.

---

3 Footnote: Pure English of Petrarch's time.

JOHN MILTON

MILTON'S ITALIAN POEMS

The Italian scholar will understand that the retention of the feminine rimes in translation from this language is an impossibility.

I

O Lady fair, whose honoured name doth grace
Green vale and noble ford of Rheno's stream –
Of all worth void the man I surely deem
Whom thy fair soul enamoureth not apace,
When softly self-revealed to time and space
By actions sweet with which thy will doth teem,
And fair gifts that Love's bow and arrows seem –
But are the flowers that crown thy perfect race.
When thou dost lightsome talk or gladsome sing, –
A power to draw the hill-trees, rooted hard –
The doors of eyes and ears let that man keep
Who knows himself unworthy thy regard!
Grace from above alone him help can bring
That Passion in his heart strike not too deep.

II

As in the twilight brown, on hillside bare,
Useth to go the little shepherd maid,
Watering some strange fair plant, poorly displayed,
Ill thriving in unwonted soil and air
Far from its native springtime's genial care;
So on my ready tongue hath Love assayed
In a strange speech to wake new flower and blade,
While I of thee, proud yet so debonair,
Sing songs whose sense is to my people lost –
Yield the fair Thames, and the fair Arno gain.
Love willed it so, and I, at others' cost,
Already knew Love never willed in vain:
Would my heart slow and bosom hard were found
To him who plants from heaven so fair a ground!

III

CANZONE

Ladies, and youths that in their favour bask,
With mocking smiles come round me: Prithee, why,
Why dost thou with an unknown language cope,
Love-riming? Whence thy courage for the task?
Tell us – so never frustrate be thy hope,
And the best thought still to thy thinking fly!
Thus me they mock: Thee other streams, they cry,
Thee other shores, another sea demands
Upon whose verdant strands
Are budding, even this moment, for thy hair
Immortal guerdon, bays that will not die:
An over-burden on thy back why bear? –
Song, I will tell thee; thou for me reply:
My lady saith – and her word is my heart –
This is Love's mother-tongue, and fits his part.

IV

Diodati – and I muse to tell the tale –
This stubborn I, that Love was wont despise
And make a laughter of his snares, unwise,
Am fallen – where honest feet will sometimes fail.
Not golden tresses, not a cheek vermeil,
Dazzle me thus; but, in a new-world guise,
A foreign Fair my heart beatifies –
With mien where high-souled modesty I hail;
Eyes softly splendent with a darkness dear;
A speech that more than one tongue vassal hath;
A voice that in the middle hemisphere
Might make the tired moon wander from her path;
While from her eyes such gracious flashes shoot
That stopping hard my ears were little boot.

V

Certes, my lady sweet, your blessed eyes –
It cannot be but that they are my sun;
As strong they smite me as he smites upon
The man whose way o'er Libyan desert lies,
The while a vapour hot doth me surprise
From that side springing where my pain doth won:
Perchance accustomed lovers – I am none
And know not – in their speech call such things sighs:
A part shut in, sore vexed, itself conceals,
And shakes my bosom; part, undisciplined,
Breaks forth, and all around to ice congeals;
But that which to mine eyes the way doth find,
Makes all my nights in silent showers abound,
Until my dawn[4] returns, with roses crowned.

4 Footnote: *Alba* – where I suspect a hint at the lady's name.

VI

A modest youth, in love a simpleton,
When to escape myself I seek and shift,
Lady, I of my heart the humble gift
Vow unto thee. In trials many a one,
True, brave, I've found it, firm to things begun;
By gracious, prudent, worthy thoughts uplift.
When roars the great world, in the thunder-rift,
Its own self, armour adamant, it will don,
From chance and envy as securely barred,
From fears and hopes that still the crowd abuse,
As inward gifts and high worth coveting,
And the resounding lyre, and every Muse:
There only wilt thou find it not so hard
Where Love hath fixed his ever cureless sting.

Beauties, Beasts, and Enchantment

CLASSIC FRENCH FAIRY TALES

Translated and with an Introduction
by Jack Zipes

A collection of 36 classic French fairy tales translated by renowned writer Jack Zipes. *Cinderella, Beauty and the Beast, Sleeping Beauty* and *Little Red Riding Hood* are among the classic fairy tales in this amazing book.

Includes illustrations from fairy tale collections.

Jack Zipes has written and published widely on fairy tales.

'Terrific... a succulent array of 17th and 18th century 'salon' fairy tales'
- *The New York Times Book Review*

'These tales are adventurous, thrilling in a way fairy tales are meant to be... The translation from the French is modern, happily free of archaic and hyperbolic language... a fine and sophisticated collection' - *New York Tribune*

'Enjoyable to read... a unique collection of French regional folklore' - *Library Journal*

'Charming stories accompanied by attractive pen-and-ink drawings' - *Chattanooga Times*

Introduction and illustrations   612pp.   ISBN 9781861712510 Pbk   ISBN 9781861713193 Hbk

Life, Life
Selected Poems

Arseny Tarkovsky

translated and edited by Virginia Rounding

Arseny Tarkovsky is the neglected Russian poet, father of the acclaimed film director Andrei Tarkovsky. This new book gathers together many of Tarkovsky's most lyrical and heartfelt poems, in Rounding's clear, new translations. Many of Tarkovsky's poems appeared in his son's films, such as *Mirror, Stalker, Nostalghia and The Sacrifice*. There is an introduction by Rounding, and a bibliography of both Arseny and Andrei Tarkovsky.

Bibliography and notes 124pp 3rd ed ISBN 9781861712660 Hbk ISBN 9781861711144

In the Dim Void

Samuel Beckett's Late Trilogy:
Company, Ill Seen, Ill Said and
Worstward Ho

by Gregory Johns

This book discusses the luminous beauty and dense, rigorous poetry of Samuel Beckett's late works, *Company, Ill Seen, Ill Said* and *Worstward Ho*. Gregory Johns looks back over Beckett's long writing career, charting the development from the *Molloy-Malone Dies-Unnamable* trilogy through the 'fizzles' of the 1960s to the elegiac lyricism of the *Company* series. Johns compares the trilogy with late plays such as *Ghosts, Footfalls* and *Rockaby*.

Bibliography, notes. Illustrated. 120pp
ISBN 9781861712974 Pbk and ISBN 9781861712608 Hbk
9781861713407 E-book

CRESCENT MOON PUBLISHING

web: www.crmoon.com e-mail: cresmopub@yahoo.co.uk

ARTS, PAINTING, SCULPTURE

The Art of Andy Goldsworthy
Andy Goldsworthy: Touching Nature
Andy Goldsworthy in Close-Up
Andy Goldsworthy: Pocket Guide
Andy Goldsworthy In America
Land Art: A Complete Guide
The Art of Richard Long
Richard Long: Pocket Guide
Land Art In the UK
Land Art in Close-Up
Land Art In the U.S.A.
Land Art: Pocket Guide
Installation Art in Close-Up
Minimal Art and Artists In the 1960s and After
Colourfield Painting
Land Art DVD, TV documentary
Andy Goldsworthy DVD, TV documentary
The Erotic Object: Sexuality in Sculpture From Prehistory to the Present Day
Sex in Art: Pornography and Pleasure in Painting and Sculpture
Postwar Art
Sacred Gardens: The Garden in Myth, Religion and Art
Glorification: Religious Abstraction in Renaissance and 20th Century Art
Early Netherlandish Painting
Leonardo da Vinci
Piero della Francesca
Giovanni Bellini
Fra Angelico: Art and Religion in the Renaissance
Mark Rothko: The Art of Transcendence
Frank Stella: American Abstract Artist
Jasper Johns
Brice Marden
Alison Wilding: The Embrace of Sculpture
Vincent van Gogh: Visionary Landscapes
Eric Gill: Nuptials of God
Constantin Brancusi: Sculpting the Essence of Things
Max Beckmann
Caravaggio
Gustave Moreau
Egon Schiele: Sex and Death In Purple Stockings
Delizioso Fotografico Fervore: Works In Process 1
Sacro Cuore: Works In Process 2
The Light Eternal: J.M.W. Turner
The Madonna Glorified: Karen Arthurs

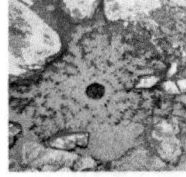

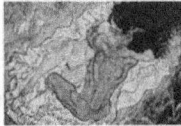

LITERATURE

J.R.R. Tolkien: The Books, The Films, The Whole Cultural Phenomenon
J.R.R. Tolkien: Pocket Guide
Tolkien's Heroic Quest
The *Earthsea* Books of Ursula Le Guin
Beauties, Beasts and Enchantment: Classic French Fairy Tales
German Popular Stories by the Brothers Grimm
Philip Pullman and *His Dark Materials*
Sexing Hardy: Thomas Hardy and Feminism
Thomas Hardy's *Tess of the d'Urbervilles*
Thomas Hardy's *Jude the Obscure*
Thomas Hardy: The Tragic Novels
Love and Tragedy: Thomas Hardy
The Poetry of Landscape in Hardy

Wessex Revisited: Thomas Hardy and John Cowper Powys
Wolfgang Iser: Essays and Interviews
Petrarch, Dante and the Troubadours
Maurice Sendak and the Art of Children's Book Illustration
Andrea Dworkin

Cixous, Irigaray, Kristeva: The *Jouissance* of French Feminism
Julia Kristeva: Art, Love, Melancholy, Philosophy, Semiotics and Psychoanalysis
Hélène Cixous I Love You: The *Jouissance* of Writing
Luce Irigaray: Lips, Kissing, and the Politics of Sexual Difference
Peter Redgrove: Here Comes the Flood
Peter Redgrove: Sex-Magic-Poetry-Cornwall
Lawrence Durrell: Between Love and Death, East and West
Love, Culture & Poetry: Lawrence Durrell
Cavafy: Anatomy of a Soul

German Romantic Poetry: Goethe, Novalis, Heine, Hölderlin
Feminism and Shakespeare
Shakespeare: Love, Poetry & Magic
The Passion of D.H. Lawrence
D.H. Lawrence: Symbolic Landscapes
D.H. Lawrence: Infinite Sensual Violence
Rimbaud: Arthur Rimbaud and the Magic of Poetry
The Ecstasies of John Cowper Powys

Sensualism and Mythology: The Wessex Novels of John Cowper Powys
Amorous Life: John Cowper Powys and the Manifestation of Affectivity (H.W. Fawkner)
Postmodern Powys: New Essays on John Cowper Powys (Joe Boulter)
Rethinking Powys: Critical Essays on John Cowper Powys
Paul Bowles & Bernardo Bertolucci
Rainer Maria Rilke
Joseph Conrad: *Heart of Darkness*
In the Dim Void: Samuel Beckett
Samuel Beckett Goes into the Silence
André Gide: Fiction and Fervour
Jackie Collins and the Blockbuster Novel

Blinded By Her Light: The Love-Poetry of Robert Graves
The Passion of Colours: Travels In Mediterranean Lands
Poetic Forms

POETRY

Ursula Le Guin: Walking In Cornwall
Peter Redgrove: Here Comes The Flood
Peter Redgrove: Sex-Magic-Poetry-Cornwall
Dante: Selections From the Vita Nuova
Petrarch, Dante and the Troubadours
William Shakespeare: Sonnets
William Shakespeare: Complete Poems
Blinded By Her Light: The Love-Poetry of Robert Graves
Emily Dickinson: Selected Poems
Emily Brontë: Poems
Thomas Hardy: Selected Poems
Percy Bysshe Shelley: Poems
John Keats: Selected Poems
Joh n Keats: Poems of 1820
D.H. Lawrence: Selected Poems
Edmund Spenser: Poems
Edmund Spenser: Amoretti
John Donne: Poems
Henry Vaughan: Poems
Sir Thomas Wyatt: Poems
Robert Herrick: Selected Poems
Rilke: Space, Essence and Angels in the Poetry of Rainer Maria Rilke
Rainer Maria Rilke: Selected Poems
Friedrich Hölderlin: Selected Poems
Arseny Tarkovsky: Selected Poems
Arthur Rimbaud: Selected Poems
Arthur Rimbaud: A Season in Hell
Arthur Rimbaud and the Magic of Poetry
Novalis: Hymns To the Night
German Romantic Poetry
Paul Verlaine: Selected Poems
Elizaethan Sonnet Cycles
D.J. Enright: By-Blows
Jeremy Reed: Brigitte's Blue Heart
Jeremy Reed: Claudia Schiffer's Red Shoes
Gorgeous Little Orpheus
Radiance: New Poems
Crescent Moon Book of Nature Poetry
Crescent Moon Book of Love Poetry
Crescent Moon Book of Mystical Poetry
Crescent Moon Book of Elizabethan Love Poetry
Crescent Moon Book of Metaphysical Poetry
Crescent Moon Book of Romantic Poetry
Pagan America: New American Poetry

MEDIA, CINEMA, FEMINISM and CULTURAL STUDIES

J.R.R. Tolkien: The Books, The Films, The Whole Cultural Phenomenon
J.R.R. Tolkien: Pocket Guide
The *Lord of the Rings* Movies: Pocket Guide
The Cinema of Hayao Miyazaki
Hayao Miyazaki: *Princess Mononoke*: Pocket Movie Guide
Hayao Miyazaki: *Spirited Away*: Pocket Movie Guide
Tim Burton : Hallowe'en For Hollywood
Ken Russell
Ken Russell: *Tommy*: Pocket Movie Guide
The Ghost Dance: The Origins of Religion
The Peyote Cult
Cixous, Irigaray, Kristeva: The *Jouissance* of French Feminism
Julia Kristeva: Art, Love, Melancholy, Philosophy, Semiotics and Psychoanalysis
Luce Irigaray: Lips, Kissing, and the Politics of Sexual Difference
Hélene Cixous I Love You: The *Jouissance* of Writing
Andrea Dworkin
'Cosmo Woman': The World of Women's Magazines
Women in Pop Music
HomeGround: The Kate Bush Anthology
Discovering the Goddess (Geoffrey Ashe)
The Poetry of Cinema
The Sacred Cinema of Andrei Tarkovsky
Andrei Tarkovsky: Pocket Guide
Andrei Tarkovsky: *Mirror*: Pocket Movie Guide
Andrei Tarkovsky: *The Sacrifice*: Pocket Movie Guide
Walerian Borowczyk: Cinema of Erotic Dreams
Jean-Luc Godard: The Passion of Cinema
Jean-Luc Godard: *Hail Mary*: Pocket Movie Guide
Jean-Luc Godard: *Contempt*: Pocket Movie Guide
Jean-Luc Godard: *Pierrot le Fou*: Pocket Movie Guide
John Hughes and Eighties Cinema
Ferris Bueller's Day Off: Pocket Movie Guide
Jean-Luc Godard: Pocket Guide
The Cinema of Richard Linklater
Liv Tyler: Star In Ascendance
Blade Runner and the Films of Philip K. Dick
Paul Bowles and Bernardo Bertolucci
Media Hell: Radio, TV and the Press
An Open Letter to the BBC
Detonation Britain: Nuclear War in the UK
Feminism and Shakespeare
Wild Zones: Pornography, Art and Feminism
Sex in Art: Pornography and Pleasure in Painting and Sculpture
Sexing Hardy: Thomas Hardy and Feminism

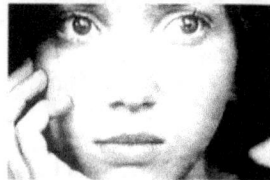

The Light Eternal is a model monograph, an exemplary job. The subject matter of the book is beautifully organised and dead on beam. (Lawrence Durrell)
It is amazing for me to see my work treated with such passion and respect. (Andrea Dworkin)

CRESCENT MOON PUBLISHING
P.O. Box 1312, Maidstone, Kent, ME14 5XU, Great Britain. www.crmoon.com

cresmopub@yahoo.co.uk   www.crescentmoon.org.uk

www.ingramcontent.com/pod-product-compliance
Lightning Source LLC
LaVergne TN
LVHW022324080426
835508LV00013BA/1313